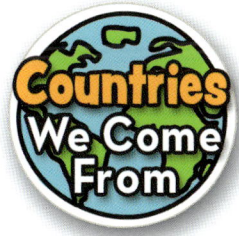

Countries We Come From

Bolivia

by Meish Goldish

Consultant: Marjorie Faulstich Orellana, PhD
Professor of Urban Schooling
University of California, Los Angeles

BEARPORT
PUBLISHING

New York, New York

Credits

Cover, © Antonio_Diaz/iStock and © Diego Grandi/Shutterstock; TOC, © Ammit Jack/Shutterstock; 4, © mezzotint/Shutterstock; 5L, © david sanger photography/Alamy; 5R, © Agatha Kadar/Shutterstock; 7, © Starcevic/iStock; 8, © Galyna Andrushko/Shutterstock; 9T, © Anna Gam/Shutterstock; 9B, © gcoles/iStock; 10, © mezzotint/Shutterstock; 11, © Dan Breckwoldt/Shutterstock; 12T, © marktucan/iStock; 12B, © wrangel/iStock; 13T, © aaltair/Shutterstock; 13B, © Coulanges/Shutterstock; 14L, © saiko3p/Shutterstock; 14–15, © Byelikova Oksana/Shutterstock; 16, © Prisma Archivo/Alamy; 17T, © Le Pictorium/Alamy; 17B, © Realy Easy Star/Alamy; 18L, © Onfokus/iStock; 18–19, © sara_winter/iStock; 20T, © iPics/Shutterstock; 20B, © Florian Kopp/imageBROKER/AGE Fotostock; 21, © Florian Kopp/imageBROKER/AGE Fotostock; 22, © urosr/iStock; 23, © Sjors737/Dreamstime; 24, © hadynyah/iStock; 25L, © Ildi Papp/Shutterstock; 25R, © Ruslana Iurchenko/Shutterstock; 26L, © Alexander Mychko/Dreamstime; 26–27, © Xinhua/Alamy; 28, © Curioso/Shutterstock; 29, © David Mercado/Reuters/Newscom; 30T, © sunsinger/Shutterstock, © vkilikov/Shutterstock, and © elnavegante/Shutterstock; 30B, © Yaroslaff/Shutterstock; 31 (T to B), © Florian Blümm, © Diego Grandi/Shutterstock, © Rawpixel.com/Shutterstock, © Free Wind 2014/Shutterstock, © Vlad Karavaev/Shutterstock, © Noradoa/Shutterstock, and © Benedikt Juerges/Shutterstock; 32, © spatuletail/Shutterstock.

Publisher: Kenn Goin
Senior Editor: Joyce Tavolacci
Creative Director: Spencer Brinker
Design: Debrah Kaiser
Photo Researcher: Thomas Persano

Library of Congress Cataloging-in-Publication Data

Names: Goldish, Meish, author.
Title: Bolivia / by Meish Goldish.
Description: New York, New York: Bearport Publishing Company, Inc., [2020] | Series: Countries we come from | Includes bibliographical references and index.
Identifiers: LCCN 2019010071 (print) | LCCN 2019010417 (ebook) | ISBN 9781642805888 (ebook) | ISBN 9781642805345 (library binding)
Subjects: LCSH: Bolivia—Juvenile literature.
Classification: LCC F3308.5 (ebook) | LCC F3308.5 .G64 2020 (print) | DDC 984—dc23
LC record available at https://lccn.loc.gov/2019010071

For more information, write to Bearport Publishing Company, Inc., 45 West 21st Street, Suite 3B, New York, New York 10010. Printed in the United States of America.

10 9 8 7 6 5 4 3 2 1

Contents

This Is Bolivia

Soaring

Joyful

Amazing

Bolivia is a large country in South America.

It's nearly as big as Texas and California combined!

Arctic Ocean

NORTH AMERICA

California

Texas

EUROPE

ASIA

Atlantic Ocean

AFRICA

Pacific Ocean

Pacific Ocean

SOUTH AMERICA

Indian Ocean

AUSTRALIA

N

W E

S

Southern Ocean

ANTARCTICA

Bolivia

About 11 million people live in Bolivia.

Bolivia has different kinds of land.

The Andes Mountains rise high in the west.

Valleys and grasslands lie in the south and east.

Thick rain forests fill the north.

The mighty Amazon River runs through Bolivia. It's one of the longest rivers in the world!

Between Bolivia's tall mountains is Lake Titicaca (tih-tih-KAH-kah).

It's the biggest lake in South America.

It sits at 12,507 feet (3,812 m) above sea level!

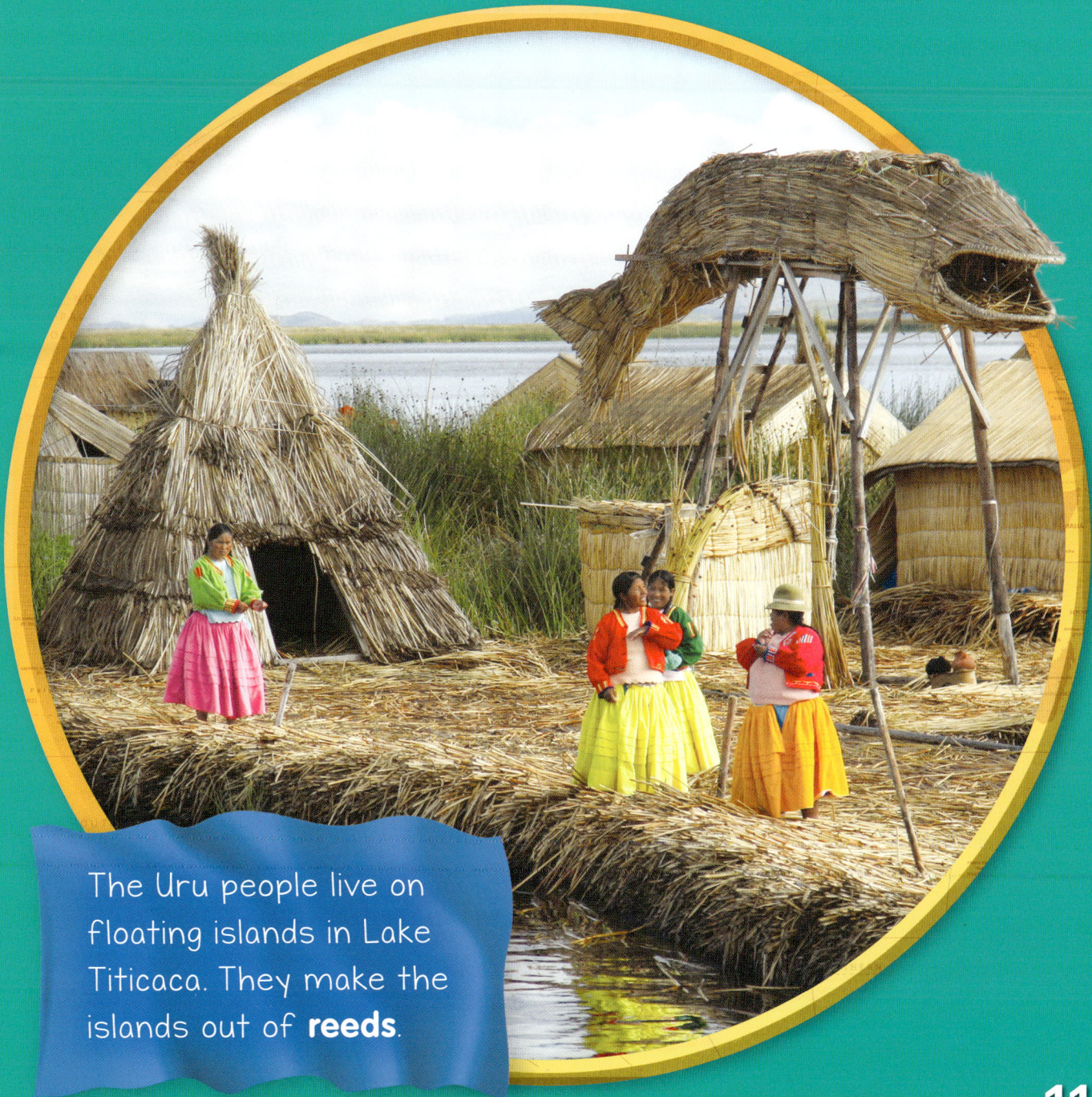

The Uru people live on floating islands in Lake Titicaca. They make the islands out of **reeds**.

Fascinating animals are found in Bolivia.

Furry llamas roam the cold mountains.

Jaguars and tapirs live in the rain forests.

tapir

Pink dolphins swim
in the Amazon River.

The huge Andean
condor is Bolivia's
national bird.

Bolivia has two **capital** cities—La Paz and Sucre (SOO-kre).

The president and lawmakers work in La Paz.

Sucre is home to Bolivia's most powerful court.

the court building in Sucre

La Paz sits over 2 miles (3.2 km) above sea level. It's the highest capital city in the world!

Native people have lived in Bolivia for thousands of years.

The Incas ruled in the 1400s.

In 1538, Spain took control of the land.

The Spanish killed many native people.

an Incan ruler and Spanish explorers

Bolivia is named after Simón Bolivar.

In the 1800s, Simón Bolivar led the fight for the country's **independence**. Bolivia became a free country in 1825.

Bolivia's Salar de Uyuni (SAH-lar day OW-oo-nee) is the world's biggest **salt flat**.

It stretches 6,500 square miles (10,460 sq km)!

After it rains, the sky reflects on the flat, wet ground!

The Luna Salada Hotel is built with blocks of salt. It's located in the salt flat. Even the furniture is made from salt!

Bolivians have many different jobs.

Farmers grow potatoes, coffee beans, and cotton.

They also raise llamas and sheep for wool.

In cities, people work in restaurants, airports, and hotels.

Other people **mine** for gold and silver.

Most people in Bolivia speak Spanish.

This is how you say *please* in Spanish:

Por favor (POHR fah-VOR)

This is how you say *thank you*:

Gracias
(GRAH-see-uhs)

Native groups in Bolivia speak over 35 other languages! The two largest groups are the Quechuas and Aymaras.

Bolivians love to eat *salteñas* (sawl-TEN-yahs).

They're pies stuffed with meat and vegetables. *Yum!*

salteñas

Another favorite dish is *plato paceño* (PLAH-toh pah-SEN-yoh).

It's a tasty mix of corn, beans, and potatoes.

Bolivians often flavor their food with *llajua* (YAH-khwah). It's a type of hot sauce.

llajua

25

It's time to have fun! Bolivians celebrate *Carnaval* in spring. People dress in wild costumes and party in the streets.

Independence Day is August 6. Bolivians celebrate their country's freedom.

What sport do Bolivians love most?
Soccer!

Many people also enjoy *fulbito*.

It's a type of soccer played on
a basketball court.

The female wrestlers are known as the Flying Cholitas.

Another popular sport is female wrestling! The women wrestle to show that they're equal to men.

29

Fast Facts

Capital cities:
La Paz and Sucre

Population of Bolivia:
About 11 million

Main language:
Spanish

Money: Boliviano

Major religion: Catholic

Neighboring countries include:
Argentina, Brazil, Chile, Paraguay, and Peru

Cool Fact: In La Paz, workers in zebra costumes help children cross the street! They also teach kids about road safety.

capital (KAP-uh-tuhl) the city where a country's government is based

independence (in-duh-PEN-duns) freedom from outside control

mine (MINE) to dig for natural resources, such as gold or silver

native (NAY-tiv) belonging to a particular place

reeds (REEDZ) types of grasses that grow in water or marshy ground

salt flat (SAWLT FLAT) a long, flat area of land that's filled with salt

31

Index

Read More

Owings, Lisa. *Bolivia (Exploring Countries).* Minnetonka, MN: Bellwether (2014).

Yomtov, Nel. *Bolivia (Enchantmant of the World).* New York: Children's Press (2019).

Learn More Online

To learn more about Bolivia, visit
www.bearportpublishing.com/CountriesWeComeFrom

About the Author

Meish Goldish lives in New York. He has written over 300 books for children.